I
Love
Insects

Lizzy Rockwell

I Like to Read®

HOLIDAY HOUSE • NEW YORK

I love insects!

I hate insects!

Insects are so pretty.

Look at the pretty butterflies.

Insects are so ugly!
Look at the flea.

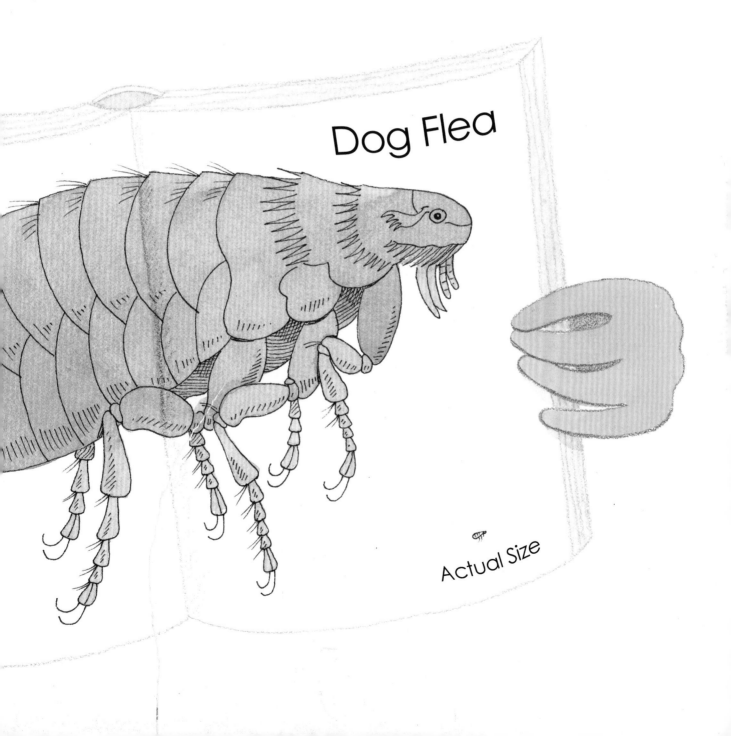

Dog Flea

Actual Size

Insects help plants.

Bees carry pollen.

This helps plants to grow.

Ants dig in the dirt.
This also helps plants.

Some insects hurt plants!

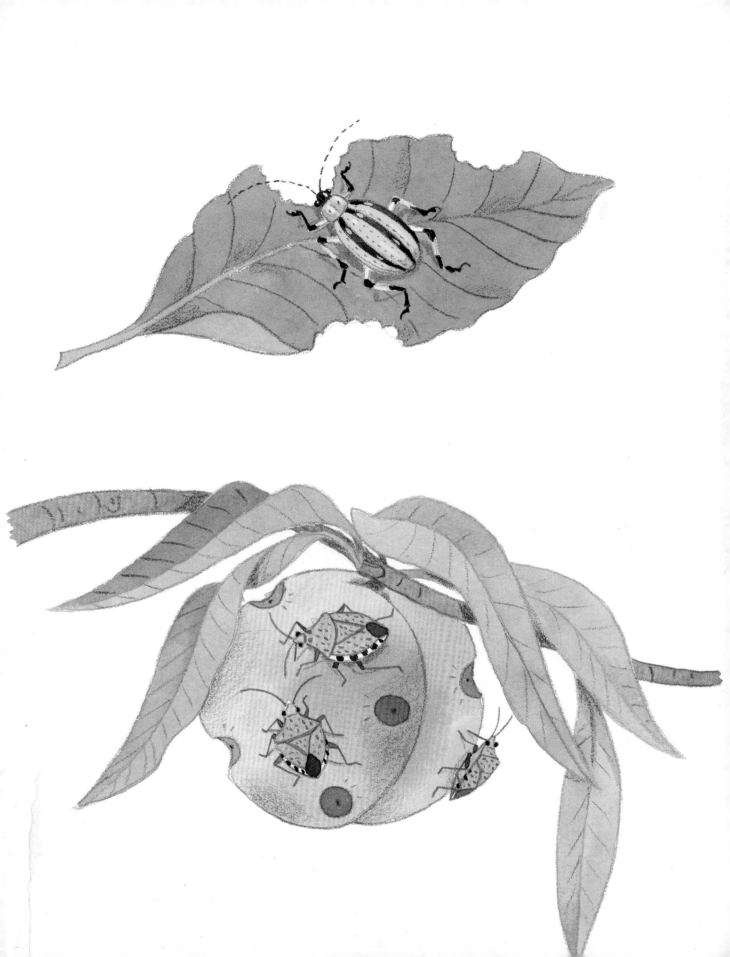

But insects have to eat too.
Some insects eat other insects.

Insects are food for many animals.

Insects make nice sounds.
Chirp! Chirp!

Insects make bad sounds!
Buzz! Buzz!

I like to look at them up close.

I want to be far away.
What if one stings me?

This one won't sting you.
She eats other insects.

In a zip, she'll be gone.

I love insects.

Do you?

Did you see these insects in this book?

Mosquito

Bumble Bee

Japanese Beetle

Ladybug

Monarch Butterfly

Cucumber Beetle

Field Cricket

Aphid

Firefly

Praying Mantis

Spring Azur Butterfly

Ant

Little Wood Satyr Butterfly

Dog Flea

Stink Bug

Tiger Swallowtail Butterfly

Housefly

Io Moth

Damselfly

Sulphur Butterfly

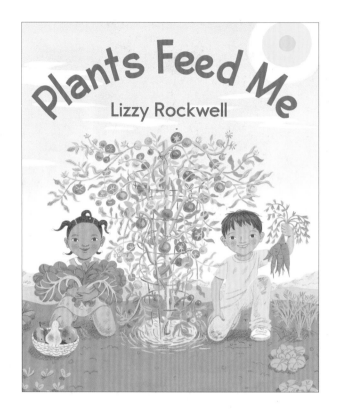

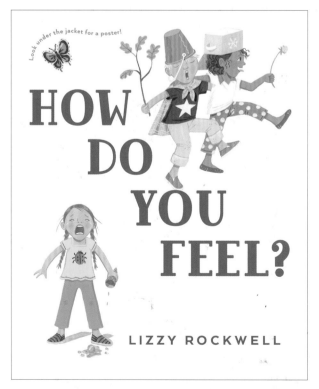